D1167379

More Praise for *City of Incandescent Light*

Matt McBride has made a potent stew of precisely recurring imagery: sheep, bones, pears, divorcees.... The poems are arranged like seasons—as they appear, they reappear, the oft-recycled titles symbolize the poet's civilized and changeless despair, unassuaged by the garnish of time known as calendar.

His is a world in which humans endure the paradox of loving each other into divorcing each other, of making "cities" of multiple selves only to enclose the single self in solitude, of creating art as a means of posthumous haunting.

The poet's final plea, "don't bury me deep," is the perfect bookend to the transparent, fragile and vulnerable "glass" life under the lights. McBride's lights are there to underscore the darkness—and this is the book's core theme—it is the darkness that is peopled, not the architectured city. Darkness is where warmth is possible, thought is quiet, night is real, and dreams are safe from "commercials."

City of Incandescent Light is so fascinatingly depressing that it comes across as playful. It is a horrible, ironic playfulness, yet edifyingly genuine, capturing the essence of a broken existence in a "full-circle" universe. McBride as commentator of this perennial journey gives us a language of heartbreaking apathy, both harrowing and irresistible. Read with caution: this is a poetry that doesn't ring twice.

—Larissa Szporluk

City of Incandescent Light

Matt McBride

Black
Lawrence
Press

Black
Lawrence
Press

www.blacklawrence.com

Executive Editor: Diane Goettel
Book and Cover Design: Amy Freels
Cover Art:"Tourism Is Alive and Well #23" by Kevin Charles Kline

Copyright © 2018 Matt McBride
ISBN: 978-1-62557-996-6

All rights reserved. Except for brief quotations in critical articles or reviews, no part of this book may be reproduced in any manner without prior written permission from the publisher: editors@blacklawrencepress.com

Published 2018 by Black Lawrence Press.
Printed in the United States.

for C.A. Diltz and Richard McBride

Contents

I

CITY OF PROGRESS

Each day another building
materializes: a post-urban
themed burrito restaurant,
a payday loan kiosk,
an abandoned gas station,
shuttered in plywood.

Some believe
there's a city behind the city,
slowly revealing itself to us.

It's wondrous,
really.

We carve busts
of the lesser saviors
in Styrofoam

as eye-winged moths
beat against incandescent bulbs.

We are trying so desperately
to outnumber the dead.

CITIES SEEN ONLY IN PHOTOGRAPHS

Buried underneath a pear tree,
the suitcase holds
a transcript of your life.

Glass replicas
replace your organs.

A breviary written on cellophane.

The thimble on your nightstand
is a radio for the ocean.

TWENTY FIFTEEN

After our last session
with the marriage counselor,

we found a skeleton
bleaching on the river's lip.

The trouble was
our dreams were commercials

in the end.
It was only a deer—

died crossing the river
before it froze.

After the police left we joked
about being a divorced,
private detective duo.

It was 2015
for the first time in history,

and we stumbled like prom dates
on new hooves.

AUTOPSY PROCTOR

Note the silliness of skin, its pettiness and shame. Thirty minutes with a cheese grater and you'll be on to fresher fruit. You'll need an electric saw for the church of ribs. See how bone dusts to cloud. Now, unclasp the heart. It will feel like a knot of fish. Take the sad thumb of tongue as well. Save. Afterwards, the throat should be easy. Observe the bridge of the larynx, how like a wishbone it was.

CITY OF THE VULNERABLE

You carry a sharpened melon baller
and portion yourself to every stranger.

You watch 8-mm films of the rain
on bedroom walls.

The dome light of every car
stays on 'til dusk.

Dandelions dispense Chinese fortunes,
things like *In less than a decade*
no one will remember what cottage cheese is,
or *Each man is a half-open door*
leading to a room for everyone.

Satellites keep catching in the trees
and periodically
need to be poked out
with broom sticks.

Every picture is of you,
bitten by sheep.

CITY OF THE ADVERTISERS

We keep handfuls of clean teeth
in pant pockets.

Lawns are bleached eye white.

The milk
is really glue.

Nightly
our president calls,

saying, *please
feel you are wanted*

*even if you aren't wanted
most of the time.*

TWENTY FIFTEEN

Because some years count double.
Because we were bobbing for apples
in gasoline.
Because it felt like
I was wearing concrete dentures.
Because I'd spent most of the year as a pearl
in the throat of a 747.
Because the subtitles
didn't match the dialogue anymore.
Because I'd waited on the tarmac
more than three hours
and now had to deplane.
Because I struggled to find words
to say after "because."
Because there was nothing we could do
for the first time anymore.
Because our divorce barely lasted longer
than the lifespan of a bee
but would soon move on:
a guinea pig, a parakeet,
us.
Because I hoped
you would be holding a sign
for me at the airport.

CITY OF MOTELS

On a taupe chair
with no definitive edges,
you watch clouds clot,

contemplate a 1992
lost to rewinding VHS cassettes.

All you ever wanted
was a box big enough to hide in.

The soap is tiny
and shaped like various waterfowl.

The telephone ringing
in the other room
will be your only remainder.

CITY OF INCANDESCENT LIGHT

Oily fingerprints embroider
every surface.

The not-things
double again.

You take X-rays of yourself
to know what sleep keeps.

Inside this glass pear
is an entire sky.

TWENTY TWELVE

In the primaries,
the boys were growing into
better daughters.

There was that weird February
where nothing moved

and all those cats
with different-colored eyes.

Always, these
memory extras.

Mostly, I thought of things to say
down the necks of empty bottles.

I remember our faces
looked nothing like dinner plates.

I remember the alarm
was full of birds.

CITY OF THE SLEEPERS

From seven streetlights,
the dream pays us out—

a string that halves
our grateful vowels,

a soul-leak,
a song everyone forgot
'til it became communal.

To dream
there must be something
in the room:

our bulbous hands

like surgical gloves
swollen with Vaseline

or the smell of fresh paint
from somewhere you can't place.

CITIES OF THE PLAIN

The curling wallpaper
is sutured awkwardly
with Scotch tape.

Each year, we tear a sheet
from the Yellow Pages,
and whoever's name's longest
is president.

A slow wind whittles
the Styrofoam trees to pellets.

CITIES MADE OF RUST

A meticulously erased sky.
A riot neglected.

Our drivers,
asleep at their wheels,

sail through
an Etch-A-Sketch infrastructure.

The skin over our wrists.

The sound
turning to snow.

Every memory
a kind of wish for itself.

We walk the longest edge of ourselves,
and it's hard, sometimes,

to distinguish the television's laughter
from the fires.

TWENTY ELEVEN

Ambulances circled in loose orbit,
their sirens' Doppler
a kind of weather.

I covered whole portions
of the city in bed sheets.

I tied the arms
of every sweater together.

I watched the meek
inherit the meeker.

The intercourse of angels is light,
I said, imitating something to say.

II

CITY OF BRIDGES BURNT

All the area rugs
are horribly stained.

Our hands
small as doll hands.

The glassy rain
hardens to varnish,

making everything a kind of
advertisement for itself.

Somehow, the flies
know our names.

Somehow, one of us
got blood on the moon.

We are such delicate monsters.

ANNABELLE

I unfold the pigeons
to save for winter.

Mornings blue slightly,
and I swear
I feel you wake in me.

Lately, nuns appear
and won't leave my windows.

My hands grey from pigeon soot.

There is a pause in my mouth.
There is this poem I wrote for you,

starting with something
by one of the last painters

and ending with the lines,
meaninglessness, where do you hide
and where do you not?

CITY OF DIVORCEES

Paint-dry skin flakes
into new continents.

The biggest problem with night here
is that it's never too dark to see.

We play this game
where we call strangers,

and whoever speaks first
loses.

We are all just trying
to make it through yesterday.

CITY OF THE PETTY

We are
shawled in bruises
big as jellyfish.

A feeling our skin is too tight.

We watch the surveillance footage
like television.

Doll-sized everything.

CITIES OF GLASS HOUSES

There are only seven names,
so everyone must share.

The phonebook consists
mostly of photographs.

Shadows leave smears.

Each evening, we listen
as our sleep machines
describe what *night* was.

At least two ghosts
for every one of us.

CITIES SEEN ONLY IN PHOTOGRAPHS

747's sail backwards
through a Windex-blue sky.

A fishbowl holds every eyelash
you've lost since birth.

Sheep are ubiquitous
and small as rice.

CITY OF THE ADVERTISERS

All dreams are held in the public domain,
and no flag is small enough.

We are blasphemously pink.
We are wonderful ashamed.

A static dander
sifts from streetlamps,

and in their carbonated light,
we make such beautiful likenesses
of our likenesses.

CITY OF THE WHITES

Someone forgot to fill in our faces.

In a better world,
we'd be dolls,

and the way
we step over broken glass
would look more like dancing.

We're terrified
there's not one void

but perhaps
a tiny void for each of us.

Don't worry,
we'll keep the streets empty for you.

CITY OF THE POLICE

Something repeated
becomes either prayer or law.

I am the machine in God,
stained angel
in the surveillance's grayscale.

Inside my helmet,
crowd noise oceans.

For no particular reason,
I wear a sock-like tie.

Father read Nietzsche
to prevent crib death.

All living things are obeying things,
he read.

In dreams, I unfasten the Kevlar,
ungate my ribs
to reveal a chained, flaming heart,
and the rioters all kneel.

When the blood of Christ
wept down my spear,
I too was blessed.

CITIES MADE OF RUST

Inside of great stadiums,
we jostle.

We watch our televisions
only a few hours
before throwing them out.

We are a search party
combing a field of bodies,
looking for grass.

And halfway across the world,
the tiniest of people

throw themselves
down the stairwells
of freshly painted factories

to protect us
from our secrets.

CITY OF HANGOVER SUNDAYS

Mannequins, left outside,
fuzz with mold.

The tombstones are chalk.
In-between, inflatable sheep graze

as a copse of toddlers in pajamas
picks them up and puts them down.

Their laughter is the rain.

On the sidewalk,
glass snails
leave strings of Vaseline.

TWO THOUSAND NINE

All the animals were revealed
as animatronic.

Blackwater changed their name,
and the Blockbuster on Court Street closed.

I asked her to marry me.

There seemed to me enough
to make a world:

empty prescription bottles,
needlepoint landscapes,
acid-wash denim.

I supposed my soul
would look like me,
only made of bubble wrap.

So few of us
knew our names.

I was a good person
more often
than when I was not.

CITIES OF GLASS HOUSES

Flour sheds from the light
of a monitor's artificial sleep.

Our eyes go all pupil.

We're uncertain
who our ghosts are.

We're running out of places
to touch each other.

CITIES OF REFUGE

Everything's plaid couches and goldfishes
in cataracts of muddled water.
Everything's glued together poorly,
so little beads ossify at each seam.
Everything's roan-colored,
'84 Civic hatchbacks
with busted tape decks
where the fast-forward sticks.
Everything's jaundiced
stacks of *National Geographics.*
Everything's stored in boxes
for shoes you don't own anymore.
Everything's palsied scrawl on a postcard,
saying, *Come home,*
saying, *We promise*
never to love you again.

CITY OF INCANDESCENT LIGHT

The Salvation Armies are chock-full
of answering machines
with leftover messages.

Imaginary children
appear on your console TV.

Even the weather's outdated.

The staples
holding on your felt wings
rust a little.

CITIES OF THE PLAIN

Skeletons of birds
hang still in the sky.

Clouds go moldy.

Someone forgot to change
the bulb in the moon,

so it flickers and clicks,
keeping you from sleep.

You say your name
into a sheet of cellophane

and hold the ball of it
in the palm of the palm of your hand.

CITIES OF THE FUTURE

There are three new colors:
stalb (a toothpaste blue),

apest (a kind of
burnt-teeth yellow-black),

and mestle
(the color water is now).

Wire coat hangers
ting into each other on tree branches
like wind chimes.

The air smells all hospital.

We have a soap for our blood.
We have LCD screens for our fingernails.
We have people landfills.

We are not uncontent.

TWO THOUSAND THREE

I held the shaved gerbil
of a woman's breast.

I drank kerosene

and threw bottles in lazy arcs
at the stuttering streetlights.

I watched our sitcom president
carry his weight in children.

I was certain
the ringing in my ears
constituted a kind of soul.

CITY OF THE POLICE

Everything's coated
in the mercury backing of mirrors.

Blood draws baby fingers
under gauged eyes.

Everyone holds a tiny radio,
boiling dictations
of citizen sin.

Our shoes are shiny as pills.

Knees broken or bent,
it doesn't matter to us.

CITY OF THE WHITES

You walk spaces
immaculate as paint.

Oil doesn't stain the teacups.

Newspapers make a skin
over every surface.

The violins are strung
with human hair.

Step carefully.

If you have to ask
who the devil is,
it's you.

SOFT TARGET

Though its flues choke with sand,
the calliope still plays.

Paint peels from Styrofoam walls
of buildings in the city proper.

Street noise is audible
through tinfoil windows,

but the cars are cardboard,
engineless—

the road merely
painted on the grass.

Overhead, rusting B-52s
form a kind of mobile.

From time to time they drop pamphlets,
but the propaganda is absurd,
things like *Cortez was the last man
to speak Spanish,*
or *President Jackson owned a bridle
made of human skin.*

The animals are all diminutive:
dachshunds, least weasels,
a mess of finches.

There's coffins too,
filled mostly
with moldy cantaloupes.

TWO THOUSAND ONE

The bitch littered,
and from every window
we hung Christmas lights.
We dug the televisions up from our yards,
bronzed the howitzers,
sewed our bodies back together more tightly.
Aging undisturbed,
we made billboards of ourselves
only vaguer, happier.
We played piano
on each other's toes.
We tried to turn off the crickets,
to stop grinding our teeth.
We were the ready-to-wear dead.

SALVATION ARMY

Everywhere they lie—
a thousand sets of Russian dolls,
haphazard and mismatched.
If anyone remembers
what the war was for,
they don't let on.
There's not much to be saved really:
a handful of shells,
a vintage dinette set
in good condition,
an electric typewriter.
How do you survive
what you've already lived through?
You can't stay in love forever.
This grubby towel
will make a nice-enough flag.
Someone's got to polish
what's left of the silver.
We can't all be heroes.

TRANSMISSION FAREWELL

The listing buoy of a silo
never gets any closer.

You knot a white bandana
on a wire fence.

As you rest your palm on it,
you feel the electric hum
of a thousand voices.

It could,
for all you know,
be the equator.

You place your savings of polished rocks—
some opal, some turquoise,
even a tiger's eye—
into a shoebox,
write your name on it,
and lay it beside you.

Over a dull breeze
one note can be heard
but has held so long
you're unable
to distinguish it from silence.

It's too late.

The kids have boiled
in mother's milk,
the trees rusted
from rain.

You've been
riding a dead horse for years,
and what you wanted
you can't say.

You begin a squatter's grave,
using the weak bowl of your hands.

CITY OF INCANDESCENT LIGHT

The resistance to sleep
became sleep.

The children all
rendered for soap.

Yellow roses
strung from hangers,

turning to paper
in a closet.

The gramophones can't be turned off.

All I ever wanted
was to find you lacking.

NINETEEN NINETY NINE

Each basement was a museum
of progressively rustier stationary bikes.
You'd watch a blank VHS tape
'til it stopped
and say the first thing that came to you,
things like *paper being torn in half*
or *new tires on hot asphalt*
or *burning dog hair*
or *sssssszzzzzhhhhhaaaaa,*
and that'd be your name.
For weeks, there'd be no moon,
but then it'd come back all littered
with plastic stir sticks
& wrinkled Styrofoam cups,
promising never to leave again.
Everybody knew only three songs:
Poison's *Every Rose Has Its Thorn*
and two others.
For fun, you'd shoot holes
though the recyclables
with an air rifle.
You rode the bus for days at a time.
There was the divorced waitress
you slept with
because she said your teeth were straight,
and there was the bum who masturbated
next to you in the holding cell
and the $20 bologna sandwich
Franklin county charged you for.

There was a cassette of your mother
saying your name over and over.
Ssssszzzzzhhhhhaaaaa it said.
Ssssszzzzzhhhhhaaaaa it said.
Ssssszzzzzhhhhhaaaaa it said.

CITIES OF GLASS HOUSES

Every citizen is someone
you recognize from the plane.

Everyone has their own little moon
to carry home.

You are your better ghost.

You are a pet here too.

There are a handful of common dreams
you struggle to forget.

CITIES SEEN ONLY IN PHOTOGRAPHS

For everything, an effigy—
tree effigies,
robot effigies,
ocelot effigies,
effigy effigies.

Paper shadows
follow us like daisy chains.

We are unconscious citizens,
the elected mute.

Cotton glass,
nudity,

and sometimes
there's weather.

CITY OF MOTELS

In the neighboring room
loops a reel-to-reel,
a recording from some SoHo party
circa 1968.

Jaundiced Polaroids drift like leaves
down thick-carpeted hallways—

everywhere, these people-echoes.

At midnight
the desk clerk calls, saying,
'You' stands for
'I want myself back.'

An ice machine
mumbles its slurred Latin,

and tonight
I am the littlest prison.

I remember your hair smelled like milk.

And when it snowed,
it snowed only on your face.

STRUCTURE FIRE

Long grasses grow riotous
in wind, yelling for miles.

A throat of smoke unfurls,
pulls itself through itself

as the orchestra watches,
holding their aluminum violins.

The sky is a runny lacquer,

and the clouds beat
like footfalls

across the heart's atrium.

CITY OF DIVORCEES

We are watching scars
crawl over us like caterpillars.

We are sleeping inside
chalk outlines of ourselves.

We are hard-boiling more eggs
than could ever be necessary.

We are picking off fingers
like daisy petals.

We are sitting in theaters
after the movie has ended,
hoping to see our name in the credits.

CITY OF REGRET

Our throats turned
inside out
like gym socks.

Ovals of mold
we leave
as fingerprints.

Things not normally
made out of concrete,
made out of concrete.

YOUR TIME BETWEEN GHOSTS

Today, a satellite falls. You watch as children pull off its gold sails, leaving only a toaster-sized motor, which beeps incessantly. You came here after some sort of falling out, though struggle to remember specifics: something about a dairy farm gone bust or a pyramid scheme involving collectible plates. At last count, the stars are down seven from the previous year. You write a letter to a woman named Annabelle, an unintelligible diatribe ending with, *here's your muffled rain,* and funnel into the envelope dried flies from your sills. They're wrong—you've no more claim to memory than breath to language. Still, it's not a total wash. Though they could stand a polish, you've got two pairs of leather shoes in good condition and a fine wool suit, only a little shiny at the elbows. In your pockets, there's money to buy dry soup with enough left over to tie one on.

CITIES OF THE PLAIN

Every albino cat
started speaking Latin
as all the dolls
walked to Brazil.
The fuselages of
abandoned 747s
were stiff maggots
circling the moon.
All but seven
streetlights went dead.
We wore nametags saying
"Your Name Here,"
but never bothered
to fill them out.
We sat in plastic lawn chairs
singin' CCR's
"Someday Never Comes."

BUSHELS

Today, there's too much
blood in my body.
Even the drivers are in on it,
moving in a ragged sort of unison.
If you could split me open
and remove the offal,
I would let you,
let you fill me with your Play-Doh organs,
let you staple on the felt wings
you made for me.
People congregate in front of shops
like the awkward moment in a musical
before everyone starts into song.
Cut me anywhere.
I'll return to the ocean.

CITY OF THE DRUNKS

Everything's made of denim.

A man holds bees,
leashed with floss,
like balloons.

Time's a cancer here.

All you've got
are your midnight teeth,
the rags you pull from your stomach,
and these tiny bibles
you offer every stranger.

Your bones grow furry
as the neons whisper you through sleep.

INSIDE EVERY BIRD

is a penny
with a silhouette
of your father as an infant.

The light caught in photographs.

The silence particular to elevators.

Everything
is only a part of itself.

CITY OF THE AWKWARD MOMENT IN A MUSICAL BEFORE EVERYONE BURSTS INTO SONG

You feel like a room
filled with many empty folding chairs.

Everybody's walking parallel,
faster than necessary.

A card table
glows with mason jars;
in each a pigeon beats

as a man, drunk for the first time,
drives a stair car in circles.

You're pretty sure it's been 1997
for the past few years.

Exit planes.

Tape hiss.

Many heavy-possibles.

You put on your favorite
person face.

CITIES SEEN ONLY IN PHOTOGRAPHS

Flies read
from a plagiarized bible.

Taxidermied squirrels
are sewn onto trees.

Radio weather.
Journals of your coma summer.

Here, you are
just a stain of light.

PLEASE

And the house made of newspaper,
on fire,
and the lows of papier-mâché cows
as they watch,
and me, inside
in my finest wool suit,
and the edges of my lapels,
my frayed wig,
my cuffs, smoldering,
and the pictures, bubbling in their frames,
and you, nude,
save for the miter and chasuble,
walking towards me,
and the clef of scars I make
on your skin
as I touch you,
and even inside the fire's chatter,
the muteness rising
to the very eaves of our ribs.

CITIES LIT BY THE WANING MOON

Many were nothing but hyperbole, founded on little more than a necklace of baby teeth or an archaic leather condom excavated from the desert. And yet, they are not unimportant. In one, the eyes of does are mined. Another is made entirely of a scaffolding used to pull stars out by their roots, a kind of urban renewal for the sky. They are always seen as if seen from a distance, always vaguely European in name, like *Eustice* or *Salemica* or *Adil*. The smallest is named *Tesra*. In it, as you read this, a tar-haired adolescent dangles her legs over the rim of a well, knocking loose the silt from her heels. And tomorrow, the residents of Bacona, Oregon will notice something off in the taste of their water.

HORIZON

To hell with collective fevers.

I've worn this coward's cross too long.

Inside my transistor,
an orchestra mediates
the decay of an atom.

Isn't it time
to note the progress
of ants across my carpet?
To draw ghosts on my hands?

A place to hang catastrophes
was the only thing I wanted.

How could I die yet,
having never been in Iowa?

Cathode-bright sunlight
erodes the clouds,
making my love seem juvenile, selfish.

Come,
I'll regret anything.

CITY OF THE SLEEPERS

Birds trail yarn,
leaving maps behind
like cat's cradles.

The telephone poles
are whispering crucifixes.

Rabbits cut
from your childhood blanket.

Inside you,
there is a room for me.

Half as you,
but half as we.

NINETEEN EIGHTY SEVEN

My father collected old newspapers,
put tinfoil over our windows.
The phone was disconnected,
but we got messages anyway,
the kind of things
dentures would say
after their owner died.
I was young as a bowl of cereal.
The knuckles of my mother's fingers
began to reverse themselves.
We put old carpeting on the lawn,
sat on the trunk of our Honda
and watched the B-17's land.
I said my first apology
to no one in particular.

ORPHAN OR NOT

The Roma band
sounds like a thousand trumpets
falling down a staircase.

The martial stars of fireworks
and the brunette I'm dancing with—

surely I loved her once.

A weathered octogenarian
sells aluminum violins and
rotary telephones
from his chosen alley.

A flock of origami pigeons
made from cigarette foils
breaks like a window
and regroups.

Surely I loved her once—
this sky over my train wreck.

Children chase a pair of argyle socks
over the bricks of the square

as the river chokes
with paper boats.

When I die,
don't bury me deep.

Notes

"City of the Vulnerable": The last lines of the second stanza are from Tomas Tranströmer's "The Half-Finished Heaven."

"City of the Advertisers ('We keep handfuls of clean teeth...')": The last stanza of this poem is based on a mishearing of a line from the song "Stolen Children" by Parenthetical Girls.

"City of the Sleepers ('From seven streetlights...')": Some lines of this poem are loose approximations of passages from chapter three of Jean Piaget's *The Child's Conception of the World*.

"City of the Advertisers ('All dreams are held in the public domain...')": The phrase "blasphemously pink" is from Wallace Stevens' poem "The Comedian as the Letter C."

"City of Incandescent Light ('The resistance to sleep...')": The third and fourth stanzas are based on an image from Allen Ginsberg's "Howl."

Acknowledgments

Many thanks to the editors and staff at the following publications where these poems first appeared, sometimes under different titles: *90's Meg Ryan, Anti-, Catch Up, Columbia Poetry Review, Country Music, Failbetter, Forklift, Ohio, InkNode, Interrupture, Juked, Kundrum Engine, Little Red Leaves, Meridian, New Collage, Ninth Letter, The Offending Adam, Revolution House, The Pinch, RHINO, SLAB, Smartish Pace, Strange Machine,* and *The Toledo City Paper.* The poems in this manuscript exist in part due to generous support from the Devine Fellowship for Poetry, the Ohio Arts Council, and the Writers in the Heartland Residency.

I owe Black Lawrence Press, and Diane Goettel in particular, everything. The publication of this book is the most significant event of my life so far and represents eight years' worth of work. I can never repay you all for turning this Word document into a material object.

Thanks as well to Kevin Charles Kline for giving Black Lawrence Press permission to use images from his "Tourism Is Alive and Well" series for the cover. For a full catalogue of his work see Kevinckline.com.

I am in debt to the following people who read drafts of this book or individual poems which became part of it, as well as people whose general support for my writing has been essential: Lisa Ampleman, Jarrod Armour, Eric Bliman, Karin Wraley Barbee, Matt Barbee, Joseph Benson, Marjorie Celona, Karen Craigo, Michael Czyzniejewski, Sean Thomas Daughtry, Joe DeLong, Bob Eckhart, Noah Falk, Flatsitter Artist Collective, Rebecca Morgan Frank,

Seth Fried, Cal Freeman, Tasha Fouts, Luke Gallant, Matt Hart (to whom this book owes its title), Heather Hamilton, Huang GeGe (Makily), John Hochwalt and the Hochwalt family, Manuel Iris, Mark Allen Jenkins, Gui Jin (Chara), Byron Kanoti, Les Kay, Timothy Liu, Stephen Looney, Todd Marren, Nicola Mason, Megan Martin, Kristi Maxwell, Leah McCormack, Julia Mehoke, Ixta Menchaca, Li Minru, Mariana Yante Barreto Perera, John Pinard and the Pinard family, Kate Polak, Micheal Rerick, F. Daniel Rzicznek, Natalie Shapero, Jonathan Thomas, Tarrah Torino, Brian Trapp, Brent Van Horne, Dietrick Vanderhill, Joshua Ware, Ruth Williams, and Snezana Zabic. I'd also like to acknowledge my appreciation of my extended family, both the McBrides and Diltzes, who deserve much more than this sentence. I'd like to express particular gratitude to my poetry teachers, without whom this book would not exist: Don Bogen, Kevin Griffith, Larissa Szporluk, Sharona Ben-Tov Muir, and Amy Newman. A special thanks is reserved for Tessa Mellas, who commented on more drafts than I have fingers and whose editing and encouragement made this manuscript what it is. I am also in debt to dozens of people not mentioned here. The list of everyone I owe in ways both direct and indirect is larger than a small phone book and rests on the counter of a kitchen in every city in this manuscript. Some may have forgotten their support or to some it may seem I have forgotten, but I promise I have not.

Matt McBride's work has appeared in or is forthcoming from *Another Chicago Review, Cream City Review, Columbia Poetry Review, FENCE, Forklift, Ohio, Map Literary, Ninth Letter, Packingtown Review, Smartish Pace,* and *Typo* amongst others. His chapbook, *The Space Between Stars,* won the 2007 Wick Poetry Chapbook Prize from Kent State University Press. He is the recipient of a Devine Fellowship, a Writers in the Heartland Residency, and an Ohio Arts Council Grant. He holds an MFA in poetry from Bowling Green State University and a PhD in comparative literature from the University of Cincinnati. Currently, he is a lecturer in the Department of Rhetoric at the University of Iowa. This fall, he will be joining the English faculty as an instructor at Wilson College.